GROWING *in the* FAITH

A Confirmation Course for Adults

JOHN COX

kevin mayhew

kevin mayhew

First published in Great Britain in 2015 by Kevin Mayhew Ltd
Buxhall, Stowmarket, Suffolk IP14 3BW
Tel: +44 (0) 1449 737978 Fax: +44 (0) 1449 737834
E-mail: info@kevinmayhew.com

www.kevinmayhew.com

9 8 7 6 5 4 3 2 1 0

ISBN 978 1 84867 770 8
Catalogue No. 1501468

Cover design by Rob Mortonson
© Images used under licence from Shutterstock Inc.
Edited by Nicki Copeland
Typeset by Rob Mortonson

Printed and bound in Great Britain

Contents

About the author

Having spent rather a long time at various universities including Cambridge, Oxford and the University College of Rhodesia and Nyasaland, John was ordained to a curacy in the diocese of Liverpool in 1968. He spent a second curacy in an inner-city ex-slum parish in Birmingham and became rector in the same parish. After a five-year period at Church House, Westminster where he was Senior Selection Secretary, helping to select ordinands, he was made Canon Treasurer at Southwark Cathedral and Diocesan Director of Ordinands and Post-ordination training.

Following four years as Vicar of Roehampton he moved to become Archdeacon of Sudbury in the Diocese of St Edmundsbury and Ipswich in 1995. When he retired in 2006 he was asked to be the part-time Diocesan Director of Education, a job he did for nearly four and a half years before retiring for a second time. It has been during these retirement years that John has been writing for Kevin Mayhew, in between being chair of governors at a primary academy, playing golf and enjoying river cruises.

Introduction

Confirmation has a mixed history. It has been variously viewed as: the 'second instalment' of the gift of the Holy Spirit; entry into church membership; a kind of puberty rite; the personal affirmation of vows taken on one's behalf at baptism; a requirement by bishops to give them a reason for visiting parishes; a way of being able to receive Holy Communion. In different times and different contexts they have all made a kind of sense, even good sense in those churches (e.g. the Anglican and Catholic) where confirmation is practised. According to its official website, the Church of England currently views confirmation this way:

> Confirmation marks the point in the Christian journey at which you affirm for yourself the faith into which you have been baptized and your intention to live a life of committed discipleship. This affirmation is confirmed through prayer and the laying on of hands by the confirming bishop. The Church also asks God to give you power through the Holy Spirit to enable you to live in the way of Jesus.[1]

Even this feels a little dated in those situations where adults are confirmed who have only recently been baptised, at which point they did themselves declare their faith and commitment. Be that as it may, confirmation is a significant step in the life of a person growing in faith and in their desire to be clearly acknowledged as a 'full member' of the Church. That significance is both in terms of what faith and commitment

---

1. Church of England, 'What is Confirmation': https://www.churchofengland.org/our-faith/confirmation/what-is-confirmation.aspx (accessed 10 December 2014).

mean for the person themselves and in the fact that it is made as a **public** affirmation endorsed/confirmed by the action of the bishop and the prayers of the church.

One of the reasons some churches practise adult baptism even when there has already been baptism as an infant is the importance given to a personal and public declaration of faith and commitment. Such 'second baptisms' may be viewed as theologically unorthodox and frowned upon by some church authorities, but their significance in terms of public and personal witness is clearly powerful. What confirmation means for the individual and for the church is one of the matters to be dealt with in this course.

This course has its origins in a book I wrote for Christian enquirers called *What Do Christians Believe?*[2] Having heard that the book was being used as a confirmation course, Kevin Mayhew asked me if I would be willing to produce a tailor-made course based on the book. So here it is. I have drawn on material in the book but it isn't simply a cut and paste job, and some parts of the book don't appear here at all. The book could still always be given to candidates to widen their knowledge!

I have suggested seven sessions. There's nothing sacrosanct about that number. Some will feel it is too many; some that it is too few. There is no reason why material should not be conflated or spread out to suit the local requirements. The same is true for the shape of the sessions. I have provided one way of doing it but the pattern could always be adapted.

The order of the sessions is not arbitrary but, again, there is no reason why it should not be changed. I had in my mind an order which begins with the candidate and gradually moves out in wider circles until all that is said about oneself, the Bible,

---

2. Kevin Mayhew, 2014.

prayer and the world feeds in to what we have learnt and want to say about God. It would be just as possible to do sessions one to six in reverse order. The order probably reflects an approach to theology – do we start with experience or with doctrinal statements about God? In some senses, of course, it is a false either/or. We are most likely to grow in faith through a mishmash of experience, reading, statements learnt about God, and prayer – each feeding and informing one another. But a course has to have some kind of shape, and here is one. The course concludes with a session in which candidates are encouraged to consider where they have come from and how they will continue to grow in the faith as they journey on in their discipleship and as part of the fellowship of the Church.

I have not provided a session specifically on the confirmation service. The way in which confirmation services are conducted varies significantly and it will make a considerable difference if, for example, there is a mixture of age groups and if some candidates are to be baptised as part of the service. In some cases there will be a rehearsal; in others not. The place of confirmation in relation to Holy Communion will also vary from place to place, the major difference being where candidates for confirmation have already been receiving Communion.

The content of the sessions offers a mixture of reflection on Scripture, input on the topic, prayer, questions for discussion, and activity. These are aids and prompts, not rules and regulations. Take from them what is felt to be useful and ignore what isn't. In some settings more material might have been helpful; in others, things will have to be left out to prevent the session becoming impossibly long. Much will depend on the dynamic and size of the group. The introduction to each session is purposely addressed directly to the readers who are assumed to be group members. Other material is more general.

I am an Anglican and this course is written with the Church of England and preparation for confirmation specifically in mind. But there is no reason why it shouldn't be used for any nurture group. The more the merrier.

Notes for the leader

As the person responsible for leading the Confirmation Course you are already likely to be experienced in leading study groups, nurture groups and the like. I am not trying to teach my grandmother to suck eggs (although I am not sure she ever did), but it might be useful if I suggest one or two points to be kept in mind as reminders.

The sessions

As you look at the course, or indeed as you go through it, you may feel that the material needs to be spread out to give greater opportunity for discussion and that you will need more sessions. You may feel that there is a lot of material in Session one, for example, and that it would be better to take two sessions over this topic. There is, of course, no reason why you shouldn't do this. Use it as it suits you and the group best.

Ground rules

The course is intended to be an interactive experience, not a series of lectures, so you will want the group members to be involved, to discuss and to pray together. It will inevitably mean that they will be sharing information about themselves – personal information and information about their faith, their prayer life and how they see things. To do so with honesty will mean that they will have to trust the other members of the group and have confidence that what they say isn't going to be gossiped about outside the group. So you may wish to begin the opening session (where this will be particularly important) establishing some 'ground rules'.

Here are some you might wish to consider:

a. Confidentiality – what is said in the group does not go outside it.

b. Members will treat each other and their views with courtesy, and will not be judgemental about others' opinions.

c. Listen to others as well as speak.

d. Everyone is here to learn from each other.

e. Everyone initially commits themselves to the whole course. (Of course, exceptional circumstances could arise that would prevent someone from attending a session. If someone feels they no longer wish to pursue the course and confirmation that would be a matter for discussion privately with the leader.)

There may also be other more practical ones, such as agreeing to keep to time both in arriving and in finishing.

Enabling

You will, of course, be an important resource for the group's learning, but everyone will have something that others can learn from. Don't hog the session, no matter how passionate you are about the subject and long to share your knowledge. Try to ensure everyone has at least the opportunity to speak, even the shy and reticent ones. But don't force it. It may be more difficult to gently keep the over-talkative from dominating the sessions.

Input

In each session there are Input thoughts. You will need to consider how you handle these. Group members could be invited to read them before going on to the next part of the session. You could set out the points being offered in your own words, or simply read out what is written. It is up to you.

Prayer

The sessions have opportunities for prayer together and for spontaneous prayer. Some of the group may be used to praying with other people. Some may not be and could find it difficult, at least initially. You will, of course, need to be sensitive to this.

Homework

For members to get the most out of the sessions it will be important that they are encouraged to do a little preparation before each session: to read through the Input for the next session, to reflect on the topic and to look at the Bible passages. Committees don't work effectively if material is simply tabled at a meeting: papers need to be distributed beforehand so that members have a chance to read them. It is similar with this course.

At the end of some sessions there are specific points relating to the next session – things to be done and objects to be provided. Please ensure members are aware of these points as the session will be less effective without this preparation.

Bibles

It is hoped that everyone will bring a Bible to the sessions. There can be an issue as to which version. While there is something to be said for everyone bringing the same version, it can also make for interesting discussion when more than one version is used, so long as people don't get hung up on minor matters of translation.

Practical matters

Where the sessions are held might depend on the number of people involved, although for the course to be most effective the group should not be larger than about ten. It's perhaps just worth remembering that no matter where you choose – be it the vicarage, a member's house or a room in the church – it will have nuances for the members, especially to start with. Hopefully the seating arrangement will be comfortable and not too formal, yet giving a sense both of purposeful activity and of everyone being equally important.

You will want to make your own decision about refreshment arrangements: at the beginning, halfway through or at the end; coffee and biscuits, or a meal.

If you use technical aids such as a CD player or flip charts, check beforehand that everything works.

Members of the group might be encouraged to bring a pen and notebook to the sessions.

Session one

Me

Introduction – you will find it helpful to read this before the group session

When I was in Sunday School we were always taught that 'I' is at the centre of sin and that the only way to overcome sin is to put a cross through the 'I'. The cross of Christ, not 'I', at the centre of our lives. So it may feel perverse to start a course on Growing in Faith with 'Me'. But we usually learn by starting with what we know and where we are and moving on from that. So you and where you are isn't a bad place to begin. Our direction of travel will be towards God, looking at what can help us to know more about God and to relate more fully to God.

In later sessions we'll be looking at what the Bible has to teach us, what we understand prayer to be about and what we can learn through it. We will think about the kind of world we live in and how that reveals things about God. Then we will come to a couple of sessions on what we understand about God, and conclude with a look to the future and how you will travel on as you continue to grow in the faith.

But this session is about you – a 'me' time. Before moving on you might like to reflect briefly on how you are feeling as you read that. The very phrase might attract you or appal you. Some people are very happy to talk about themselves. Others find it more difficult – they like to keep themselves to themselves. Are you aware of which kind of person you are? How does the prospect of sharing things about yourself feel?

Inevitably it will mean being honest about yourself and sharing personal matters with others, as well as listening to what they have to say about themselves. It is important that you feel comfortable with doing that, that there is an agreement of confidentiality within the group, and that you do not feel coerced to reveal anything you don't want to. It will be up to the leader of the group to manage all this.

The session asks you to share with others who you are. In *Les Miserables*, Jean Valjean has an agonising time trying to decide whether or not to reveal who he is to his old adversary Javert. He sings of that struggle in a song entitled 'Who am I?' It concludes with him virtually shouting his name and then giving his old prisoner number. His name said who he was and how he saw himself. His number said what he was and how he was viewed by Javert.

'**Who** are you?' we're asked, and so often we say **what** we are: I'm the vicar, a teacher, a postman, a banker, a nurse. This is what we **do**, but is it who we **are**? Sometimes our work does very much shape and express who we are, but this is not the case for everyone. We might equally answer in terms of our relationships with others: I'm Jean's husband; I'm Frank's mother; I'm a grandfather; I'm a twin. Or in terms of our personality: I'm an introvert; I'm a control freak; I'm a bit shy. This is becoming more personal and perhaps more difficult. But in the privacy of your own home it is worth reflecting on who you are, and it is good also to think about what 'worth' you feel you have – to your family, to your friends, to your colleagues, to yourself, to God.

In **preparing for the session**, consider what gives you 'worth', and what undermines it. Jesus said that you are worth more than the sparrows. In fact, in his love he showed that you are worth everything (Matthew 10:31). Do you believe it?

Group session one

Opening prayer

We are in your presence, God our Father.
You are with us, the Lord of all.
We come to learn: open us to your Spirit,
show us your way, teach us your truth.

Help us to be honest with ourselves
and honest about ourselves,
to listen to each other
and to speak without judging,
that we may grow in understanding,
in trust and in faith,
for Jesus' sake.
Amen.

Welcome

The leader introduces the session.

Who I am

Activity

In pairs (if possible, of people who do not know each other well already), each member takes a turn in introducing themselves:

• Who they are

• Why they are here

• What they want to get from the course.

Each person then tells the whole group up to five significant things about their partner.

Together the group lists all the things they are looking to get out of the course.

My relationships

Activity

On a piece of paper, put yourself in the middle, and in concentric circles moving outwards, name the people you feel you have a relationship with, moving out from those who are closest to you to those who are more distant. Discuss your circles with your partner and then, if you have not done so already, add the people in the group.

As a group, discuss any points that emerged for you from this activity. What marks the difference in the relationships of those close to you from those who are more distant? List the words used. Which words would you feel are most appropriate to describe your relationship with God?

Reading

The story of the creation of man and woman is read:
Genesis 2:4b-9, 15-24:

> In the day that the Lord God made the earth and the heavens, when no plant of the field was yet in the earth and no herb of the field had yet sprung up – for the Lord God had not caused it to rain upon the earth, and there was no one to till the ground; but a stream would rise from the earth, and water the whole face of the ground – then the Lord God formed man from the dust of the ground, and breathed into his nostrils the breath of life; and the man became a living being. And the Lord God planted a garden in Eden, in the east; and there he put the man whom he had formed. Out of the ground the Lord God made to

grow every tree that is pleasant to the sight and good for food, the tree of life also in the midst of the garden, and the tree of the knowledge of good and evil.

. . . The Lord God took the man and put him in the garden of Eden to till it and keep it. And the Lord God commanded the man, 'You may freely eat of every tree of the garden; but of the tree of the knowledge of good and evil you shall not eat, for in the day that you eat of it you shall die.'

Then the Lord God said, 'It is not good that the man should be alone; I will make him a helper as his partner.' So out of the ground the Lord God formed every animal of the field and every bird of the air, and brought them to the man to see what he would call them; and whatever the man called each living creature, that was its name. The man gave names to all cattle, and to the birds of the air, and to every animal of the field; but for the man there was not found a helper as his partner. So the Lord God caused a deep sleep to fall upon the man, and he slept; then he took one of his ribs and closed up its place with flesh. And the rib that the Lord God had taken from the man he made into a woman and brought her to the man. Then the man said,

'This at last is bone of my bones
and flesh of my flesh;
this one shall be called Woman,
for out of Man this one was taken.'

Therefore a man leaves his father and his mother and clings to his wife, and they become one flesh. And the man and his wife were both naked, and were not ashamed.

Activity

This is not a scientific explanation. It is a sacred story.
What does it tell you about:

- The relationship between God and human beings?

- The relationship between men and women?

- The relationship between human beings and
  the created order?

There is another account of creation. Read Genesis 1:24-31:

> And God said, 'Let the earth bring forth living
> creatures of every kind: cattle and creeping things
> and wild animals of the earth of every kind.' And
> it was so. God made the wild animals of the earth
> of every kind, and the cattle of every kind, and
> everything that creeps upon the ground of every
> kind. And God saw that it was good.
>
> Then God said, 'Let us make humankind in our
> image, according to our likeness; and let them have
> dominion over the fish of the sea, and over the
> birds of the air, and over the cattle, and over all the
> wild animals of the earth, and over every creeping
> thing that creeps upon the earth.'
>
> So God created humankind in his image,
> in the image of God he created them;
> male and female he created them.
>
> God blessed them, and God said to them, 'Be
> fruitful and multiply, and fill the earth and subdue
> it; and have dominion over the fish of the sea and
> over the birds of the air and over every living thing
> that moves upon the earth.' God said, 'See, I have
> given you every plant yielding seed that is upon the

face of all the earth, and every tree with seed in its fruit; you shall have them for food. And to every beast of the earth, and to every bird of the air, and to everything that creeps on the earth, everything that has the breath of life, I have given every green plant for food.' And it was so. God saw everything that he had made, and indeed, it was very good. And there was evening and there was morning, the sixth day.

What does this add to your understanding about being human?

Input

As scientific knowledge advances we are learning more and more about what it is that makes us who we are. Any number of different disciplines have been drawn into the research – biochemistry, anatomy, genetics, psychology, sociology, cultural studies and so on. Sometimes such studies have implied that they are the key, and with that comes a reductionism which tends to say that we humans are **merely** this or that. Wisdom demands that we see ourselves as complex interactions of all kinds of components and influences. We are not simply our DNA, or our upbringing. We are not simply the product of our culture or climate. The discussion continues as to which shapes us most, our nature or our nurture, and how they interact. In the past a great deal of effort has been put into showing how different we are from other animals. These days we are discovering how much we have in common, especially with the other primates and great apes.

Some people find such research stimulating; others find it disturbing. Some wish to emphasise humankind as a special feature of God's creation; others marvel at the diversity but also the similarity between certain species.

The biblical stories of creation seek to account, in non-scientific terms, for the differences They do this most importantly in terms of the relationship between God and humanity, and what humans have in common, not so much with the rest of creation, but with God himself. You might wish to consider which parts of the story specifically indicate this particular relationship, such as the moulding of Adam from the dust and God's breath giving him life; the way woman was said to have been created; the place God gives to human beings in relation to the rest of creation.

Activity

Here are some definitions of human beings:

- 'A culture-bearing primate that is anatomically similar and related to the other great apes but is distinguished by a more highly developed brain and a resultant capacity for articulate speech and abstract reasoning.' (*Encyclopedia Britannica*)

- 'A naked ape' (Desmond Morris)

- 'A political animal' (Aristotle)

- 'Made in the image of God' (the Bible)

What specifically does the biblical definition add to our understanding?

Input

One way of *understanding ourselves* in relation to God is to say that it is he who calls us into being. Our task is to **respond** to this call and to live out our vocation. He makes us able to 'respond' to him, but he also calls us to be 'responsible' through the gift of choice, free will.

He calls us to be fully **human** – and the model for what that means is to be found supremely in Jesus, but also in the great saints of the church.

He calls us to fulfil our vocation to be human in terms of **relationships** – as a single person, a husband or wife, a parent or grandparent, a friend, a neighbour, a colleague, and so on.

He calls us to be **disciples** – learning followers of Jesus who are growing in maturity in the faith and in relationship with him.

He calls us to exercise our **gifts** through what we do – as carers, as workers, as stewards of creation.

Our vocation is to fulfil in all these different ways what it is God would have us **be** and **do**.

As a group, discuss how you understand this idea of 'vocation'.

Reading

When I look at your heavens, the work of your fingers,
the moon and the stars that you have established;
what are human beings that you are mindful of them,
mortals that you care for them?
Yet you have made them a little lower than God,
and crowned them with glory and honour.

Psalm 8:3-5

This makes a very big claim for what it means to be human.

Activity

Discuss as a group:

- What does this say about the 'worth' God gives to human beings?

- What does it say about the responsibility it places upon human beings?

- How far do you think human beings live up to this?

- What else gives worth to a person? What gives you worth?

In conclusion

- List what you would want to celebrate about being who you are.

- List what you would like to become.

Reflection

Just as I am, without one plea,
but that thy blood was shed for me,
and that thou bidd'st me come to thee,
O Lamb of God, I come, I come.

Just as I am, though tossed about
with many a conflict, many a doubt;
fightings and fears within, without,
O Lamb of God, I come, I come.

Just as I am, poor, wretched, blind;
sight, riches, healing of the mind,
yea, all I need, in thee to find,
O Lamb of God, I come, I come.

Just as I am, thou wilt receive;
wilt welcome, pardon, cleanse, relieve,
because thy promise I believe,
O Lamb of God, I come, I come.

Charlotte Elliott (1798–1871)

Prayer

Lord, we thank you for one another,
for the variety of gifts and insights each one brings.
We thank you for all who love and support us,
for those who value us and give us worth.

We thank you that you have called us into being,
called us to be your friends.
Be with us and hold us,
guide us and challenge us,
love us and forgive us,
in Jesus' name.
Amen.

Session two

The Bible

Introduction – you will find it helpful to read this before the group session

You may have already tried reading the Bible and found at least some of it hard going, difficult to understand, a bit weird. On the other hand, it may have been the reading of passages from the Bible that first attracted you to Christianity and made you want to find out more. You may have only heard it read in church, and enjoyed the stories but found some of the passages from St Paul's letters rather complicated. You may have heard some people speak as though every word of the Bible has to be taken as literally true, while others say it's all a load of myth and legend. Some people dismiss it; others quote from it constantly. The range of reactions to the Bible is almost limitless.

For Christians, the Bible is clearly a very important book. It's called **Holy** (the Holy Bible, or the Holy Scriptures) and it is described as the **word of God**. It has a special place of authority as the basis for so much we know about God and Jesus, for what the Church teaches and what Christians believe. It's not quite like any other book.

For a start, it's not just one book. It's a whole library of books, written over many centuries by many different people. There are 39 books in the Old Testament and 27 in the New Testament. 'Testament' means 'covenant' or 'agreement' – initially between God and his people the Jews and then, through Jesus, with the whole world.

The **Old Testament** books were originally written in Hebrew and then translated into Greek. The Greek translation was known as the Septuagint, because 70 scholars were involved in producing it. It included those books that are now known as the Apocrypha (books such as Tobit, Wisdom of Solomon, Maccabees). The Old Testament was what the early Christians would have called 'the Scriptures'.

Jews divided the Old Testament books into three main groups:

- The **Torah** (law), comprising the first five books. It was also known as the Pentateuch (and was once believed to have been written by Moses).

- The **Prophets** (books such as Isaiah, Jeremiah, Amos, Habbakuk, and also the history books such as Kings).

- The **Writings** (Psalms, Proverbs, Ezra, Nehemiah and Chronicles, etc.).

It is not possible to know precisely who wrote all these books. Many of them are edited collections of oral and written material, and some of them originated over a very long period of time.

Together, the books of the Old Testament provide a record of God's relationship with his people, Israel, from the creation of all things to a time not long before Jesus. Most important to the people of Israel were the books of the law that set out God's requirements, covering all aspects of personal and corporate life. Worship was central to the life of Israel and there were plenty of instructions regarding religious festivals and rituals, as well as liturgical material such as the Psalms.

The history of Israel is seen always in terms of the outworking of the people's relationship with God. Obedience and faithfulness were rewarded with prosperity and en-largement. Faithlessness (worshipping other gods) resulted in famines, wars, invasions and exile. It was around the time of the Exile that the prophets were prominent, delivering messages of God's judgement on the nation's wrongdoing, and offering hope in times of difficulty. Prophets were 'forth-tellers' rather than foretellers – they read the signs of the times and interpreted them in the light of their faith and the way they believed God would act.

The **New Testament** provides us with the story of Jesus, which is presented to us in the four **Gospels**. Most scholars agree that Mark was the earliest Gospel to be written and that Matthew and Luke drew upon his work and added other material of their own. John's Gospel is rather different in style and is considered to be the most 'theological' or 'spiritual' of the Gospels.

The **Acts of the Apostles** provides a picture of the life of the early Church as, guided by the Holy Spirit, the Christian faith spread through the Mediterranean world. It focuses on major figures such as St Peter and St Paul. The development of the teaching of the early Church is found in the **Epistles**, letters sent to Christian communities by St Paul and others to guide them in their understanding of what Jesus had done and how they should behave.

The final, and rather strange book, is the **Book of Revelation**, which contains a series of visions setting out what will happen in the last days when the current order of the cosmos will come to an end and there will be a 'new heaven and a new earth'.

As the early Church spread and the Church of Rome became increasingly influential, Latin translations of the Bible became the norm in Western Europe. While parts of the Bible were translated into English as early as the seventh century, and the famous Lindisfarne Gospels have an English translation alongside the Latin text, it wasn't until the fourteenth century that John Wycliffe translated the whole of the Bible into English. The setting-out of the Bible into chapters and verses did not appear until 1560, and the first authorised version in English appeared in 1611 – the King

James Bible. These days there are dozens of different translations, from scholarly to popular – e.g. the New Revised Standard Version, the Jerome Bible, the Good News Bible, *The Message*. Parts of the Bible have been translated into more than 1300 different languages.

When it comes to understanding the Bible, there are a number of general points that are worth keeping in mind:

a. The Hebrews were not particularly interested in abstract ideas. Their preferred way was to tell stories. Of course, the Bible includes much else – poems, law codes, wise sayings, hymns and letters. But story is a good place to begin.

b. We can get hung up about whether a story is true or not, especially if by 'true' we mean, 'Did it actually happen?' Truth and fact are not necessarily the same thing. It is perfectly possible to believe that the story of Jonah, for example, holds some very important truths about the way God works in spite of his servants not always doing what he wants them to do. It speaks of God's forgiveness, even when we feel revengeful. But we don't have to believe that Jonah was actually swallowed by a whale – though it does add drama to the story. And the truths remain even if Jonah never existed.

c. Jesus, who of course was a Jew, typically told stories to convey truths about God and the kingdom. It was St Paul who set out a more 'theological' way of understanding what Jesus did, what he taught and what his significance was in terms of our salvation.

d. When we read a passage from the Bible, it is worth asking:

   • **When** was this written? Most accounts, even of historical events, were not eye-witness reports.

- **Where** was it written? Does it come from an urban or a rural setting? Was it written in Palestine or in a foreign country during a time of exile?

- **For whom** was it written? Was it written for people from a Jewish or a Greek background and mindset? For example, this made a difference to the way Matthew wrote his Gospel (for a Jewish audience) and the way Luke wrote his (for a Gentile audience).

- **What** kind of writing is it? Is it a story, a poem, a love song, a piece of propaganda, a hymn or a genealogy?

- **Why** was it written? Was it written to convey scientific knowledge or truths about the human condition? Was it written to encourage a people who were in danger of losing all hope, or to remind them of God's demands? Was it written just to tell a story about someone or, more importantly, to convey the significance of that person – Jesus, for example?

You may not feel that you are in a position to answer all those questions – at least not in detail. Don't worry, the Bible will still speak to you even without all these questions being answered. But if you want to grow in the faith, digging deeper into the Bible will help. Some people find a Bible commentary helpful. Your group leader may be able to suggest one that is suitable.

Try to keep an open mind when you read the Bible – some of it will be strange, but don't write it off. Keep an open heart and let God speak to you through what you read. If there are passages you find boring – skip them. You can always come back to them later. Don't think you just have to swallow it: never be afraid to ask questions. The Bible and God are plenty big enough to stand a bit of probing!

Take it seriously. It's not for nothing that people have said that the Bible is, or contains, the word of God. It is a marvellously exciting, challenging, comforting, mysterious book that can help us grow in understanding and in our relationship with God.

In **preparing for the session**, think of a favourite biblical story or passage and what it means to you.

Group session two

Opening prayer

We are in your presence, God our Father.
You are with us, the Lord of all.
We come to learn: open us to your Spirit,
show us your way, teach us your truth.

You speak to us through your word
and we seek to learn your will.
Help us to understand the Bible,
its message and its meaning.
Through it may we learn of your activity
in the world, among nations, in communities
and in the hearts of men and women,
that we may grow in understanding,
in trust and in faith,
for Jesus' sake.
Amen.

Welcome

The leader introduces the session.

Activity

The psalmist describes God's word in this way:

> Your word is a lamp to my feet
> and a light to my path.
>
> *Psalm 119:105*

In pairs, share your favourite biblical passage. Say what you particularly like about your chosen passage and how it has thrown light on your understanding and/or guided you in the way you should live. Share together as a group what you have discussed.

Input

In the second letter to Timothy (2 Timothy 3:16), the author states that 'All scripture is inspired by God'. The Scriptures are one of the ways God shows himself to his people, instructs them, guides, encourages and challenges them. They are part of God's self-showing, the revelation of himself, which means that we are not left simply to guess what God is like, nor do we have to rely on our own cleverness to discover his purposes.

In what way might we understand how 'inspiration' works? A piece of art, a poem or a piece of music can be said to be inspired. A performance can lead critics to say that it was so marvellous it was inspired. In a rather general way it means that something is full of spirit, that a person seems to reach a quality beyond themselves.

Some people want to be much more specific when it comes to biblical inspiration – it is as though the writer was so 'taken over' by God, or by the Spirit of God, that they became merely the mechanism of conveying God's words. Some of the Old Testament prophets seem to convey this, having gone into a trance or 'mystical state' before uttering the message. The account of the 'frenzy' that Saul experienced when the spirit of God possessed him (1 Samuel 10:9-13) may well be an example of this.

Preachers sometimes say that in preparing for a sermon they spend time praying, opening themselves up to the Spirit of God and that it is God's words they speak.

Activity

Discuss together how you understand the idea of 'inspiration'.

Context

The community from which the Bible emerged was largely a rural community. It makes sense therefore to describe God as a 'shepherd' (Psalm 23:1), and for Jesus to describe himself as 'the good shepherd' (John 10:11).

- What qualities does this image convey to you?

- What equivalent image from a modern urban setting could you suggest that would convey the same or similar qualities?

- What does this tell you about the importance of context?

Inconsistencies

Does the Bible ever contradict itself? Yes. Does it ever get things wrong? Yes. It is an authoritative book – that is, it can be relied upon in the overall consistent picture it gives of being human and in the picture it builds up about God. But it is not infallible. It can get dates wrong; it can muddle up names. But through its stories and its accounts, its poetry and its wise sayings, its teaching and its visionary hope, it can inspire us, comfort us, challenge us and teach us. And in these terms it is to be trusted; it is authoritative.

There are times when accounts of the same event or versions of the same story in the Bible differ. Cynically, one might think it was simply that one or other of the writers got it wrong. But usually, especially in the New Testament, differences can be explained in terms of the meaning the writer sees the event or story having – its significance.

Reading

> Then came the day of Unleavened Bread, on which the Passover lamb had to be sacrificed. So Jesus sent Peter and John, saying, 'Go and prepare the Passover meal for us that we may eat it.' They asked him, 'Where do you want us to make preparations for it?' 'Listen,' he said to them, 'when you have entered the city, a man carrying a jar of water will meet you; follow him into the house he enters and say to the owner of the house, "The teacher asks you, 'Where is the guest room, where I may eat the Passover with

my disciples?' " He will show you a large room upstairs, already furnished. Make preparations for us there.' So they went and found everything as he had told them; and they prepared the Passover meal.

Luke 22:7-13

This passage from Luke tells of Jesus making arrangements for the Last Supper. It would be the Passover meal, when Jews remembered God's saving action in rescuing the Hebrews from Egypt (Exodus 12:1-12, 29-36). The following day, Jesus would be crucified.

John in his Gospel says that that last meal was **before** the Passover (John 13:1) and that the crucifixion happened on the day of the Passover (John 18:28, 39; 19:14).

Activity

Discuss together what you make of this and why the Gospel writers differ.

- How do you feel when you learn of such differences?

- Does it make any difference to your understanding of the authority of the Bible?

An input thought

An old Sunday School chorus declared:

> Yes, Jesus loves me,
> yes, Jesus love me,
> yes, Jesus loves me,
> the Bible tells me so.[3]

That simple chorus states that for the Christian the Bible has authority. If the Bible says something, it is true.

---

3. Refrain by William B. Bradbury (1816–1862), to a poem by Anna B. Warner (1860).

Unless we agree with those who say that every word of the Bible is literally true, we have to decide how we understand the phrase, 'The Bible is true.' Is it true when it agrees with things I already know or believe, and untrue when it doesn't? Is it true because of its general message about God's love and the saving work of Jesus? What kind of truth does it convey if it tells stories of events that we cannot accept as being literally true, such as the story of Jonah. We might say the parables of Jesus are 'true', even though the events they record never actually happened.

Activity

In pairs, discuss how each of you understands the truth of the Bible. Don't worry if you don't feel you have the 'right' answer. Risk saying what you feel is true for you — even if that is 'I don't know'.

Reflection

Lord, thy Word abideth,
and our footsteps guideth;
who its truth believeth
light and joy receiveth.

When our foes are near us,
then thy Word doth cheer us,
word of consolation,
message of salvation.

When the storms are o'er us,
and dark clouds before us,
then its light directeth,
and our way protecteth.

Who can tell the pleasure,
who recount the treasure,
by thy Word imparted
to the simple hearted?

Word of mercy, giving
succour to the living;
Word of life, supplying
comfort to the dying!

O that we, discerning,
its most holy learning,
Lord, may love and fear thee,
evermore be near thee!

William Baker (1821–1877)

Prayer

Lord, we thank you for the gift of your word,
that through the pages of the Bible
we may hear you speak to us.
But we especially thank you for the gift of your Son,
the Word, bringing us love and mercy,
forgiveness and salvation.
To you be praise, now and always.
Amen.

The next session

Members are asked to bring to the next session one object
that has special significance for them in their relationship with
a friend or a family member.

The leader of the group should provide a candle, a cross
or crucifix, an icon *(picture)* of Jesus, a CD player and some
suitable meditative music.

Session three

Prayer

Introduction – you will find it helpful to read this before the group session

At times, prayer can seem to be the most natural thing in the world. At others, it can feel strange or difficult, even pointless. If you've ever felt like that, don't worry – so have endless numbers of Christians, including the great saints. Part of the wonder of prayer – and it's difficulty – lies in the fact that as we pray we are addressing someone, something, beyond us, unseen.

Books on prayer sometimes tell us that we should think of prayer as a conversation, and there is truth in this. But when we are having a conversation we normally have the advantage of being immediately aware of the other person's reaction to what we say, and this is even true of telephone conversations. But it is not the same with God – at least not usually. As we grow in our relationship with God, including through prayer, we may discover a closeness in which the aspects of a conversation are more obviously present. But even for some faithful and prayerful people, it never happens quite like that. It is important that in seeking to grow in prayer we don't beat ourselves up with guilt because we don't feel we are 'getting it right'.

Even people who don't regard themselves as religious will often admit that on occasions they have prayed, have asked God for something. It may have been in a time of crisis or desperation when they were at their wits' end and they turned to God and asked for help – help in a time of danger, help with a broken relationship, help with a mounting debt, help with nerves before an exam. When all else fails they turn to God and ask for help. We've all done it.

It is not surprising, therefore, that it is often assumed that prayer is about **asking**. We may not be sure exactly *how* God will answer our prayer or even *if* he will answer our prayer, but we give it a try. There are plenty of people who can tell us that God has answered their prayer, sometimes in an amazing way.

There is nothing wrong with asking God for things. Jesus encouraged us to do so, and indeed even promised that if we ask we shall receive (Matthew 7:7; Luke 11:9, 10). In John's Gospel Jesus is reported as adding a brief but important condition: 'I will do whatever you ask in my name, so that the Father may be glorified in the Son. If in my name you ask me for anything, I will do it' (John 14:13, 14).

Asking in Jesus' name isn't just a matter of tagging Jesus' name on to our request; it implies asking for things and in a way that fits with what Jesus would want for us. It is the prayer that not only seeks what we want but is also in accordance with what Jesus would want for us – 'Your will be done' (Matthew 6:10). God is not a slot machine! And this may help us to understand why some of our prayers do not result in our receiving what we want. Not everything that we want would actually be the best for us. And God wants the best for us.

Because we don't always receive what we want, we can think that God doesn't care, that he won't do things we ask for, or that he simply isn't there. And then we think that prayer doesn't work. But prayer is much more than just asking for things. Prayer is also about such things as thanks, wonder, praise, saying sorry, listening and – most importantly – it is about our relationship with God.

Life may not always be easy, but for most of us there is so much to be **grateful** for. Just listen to the news and hear what others are having to endure. We aren't starving; we aren't in the middle of a violent civil war; our family hasn't been wiped out by a hurricane. There are things we possess, but more importantly there are people for whom we should be grateful –

those who love and care for us, as well as the thousands of unknown people whose work and skills make our lives possible. Thanking people is not just a politeness; it is also part of what makes us truly human. And thanking God, in whose creative love all things originate, is an important part of prayer, of our growing in spiritual maturity – perhaps especially when not everything is going well.

To see a child's look of **wonder** is a joy – that moment of rapt attention and delight that embraces the whole child. We, too, experience that – the wow moment, the occasion when an experience, a sight, an achievement gives us goosebumps. Our experience of God can bring us such moments, and our response is a prayer of wonder – even if we don't actually say anything.

It may not be a very pleasing trait if someone is always looking to be praised, but we do all need **praise**. It builds up our sense of worth and self-confidence. Offering praise to another person not only gives them a lift; it enlarges us too. Praise comes from a generosity of spirit towards others. It is not self-regarding. God doesn't *need* praise, but offering God praise is something *we* need. Praising God means that we have taken the trouble to think about God, about all that is praiseworthy in what he does and in what he is, and that we are prepared to say so.

It would be nice to think that we didn't get or do things wrong. But we do. We make mistakes; we do things that hurt others. It is what we do about it that is important. Do we pretend it didn't happen? Do we hope no one noticed? Do we bury it in a deluge of guilt? **Saying sorry** is one of the ways of dealing with what goes wrong – sorry to other people if we have hurt or neglected them, and sorry to God who knows all about us – the rotten bits as well as the good. We cannot always be sure other people will forgive us. We are not always sure we can forgive ourselves. But if we come to God in honesty and trust, not only do we grow in self-knowledge but we also grow in the knowledge that God does forgive us, as he has promised. Confession is not easy but, as the saying goes, 'it is good for the soul'.

These aspects of prayer could lead us to think that prayer is all about our speaking to God. But an important part of prayer is **listening**. Stop the chatter and be quiet, be still. If you are not used to it, silence can be 'deafening', and certainly disturbing. But attentive silence, when we focus upon God, helps us to be more aware of the presence of God and it gives God space to speak to us. Discerning what is of God and what are simply our own thoughts chasing around our head is, of course, part of what it means to be growing in mature prayer.

The point of prayer is to grow in **relationship** with God. The loving God longs for us to love him back. He invites us to be his lovers. And love is all about relationship. Our relationship with God may begin in a quite dramatic way. For others it is much more gradual. And, like all relationships, it needs working at, and over the years it will change. Prayer is one way of helping our relationship with God to grow and develop. It opens us up to God, and though it may feel that it is our work, the truth is that in prayer God is at work – in us and with us.

Not all prayer takes place when we are on our own. There are times when prayer is a **shared** experience – in a group or as part of a congregation. In an act of worship we can feel helped by the fact that our prayers are part of the prayer offered by the whole church. In a group we can sometimes feel very self-conscious if we are asked to pray; at other times it will help us not only in our relationship with God but also in our relationships with one another.

Understanding something of what prayer is about is important, but most of us actually need more help with **how to pray**. The group session will spend more time on this aspect of prayer. There are lots of helpful books on prayer, but you don't have to have read them all before you start praying. The group leader may be able to suggest such a book for you. There are similarly many thousands of books on relationships and – especially if we are going through a sticky time – they can be helpful, but it would be wrong to imagine that we cannot make perfectly good relationships without them. We may know of people who are considered to be experts in prayer, and they may well have useful things to say. But you don't have to be an 'expert' before you pray, and you certainly should not feel guilty because you aren't sure about how to pray.

Our relationship with God, like other relationships, means we need to give him **time**, and that includes prayer time. Time to be quiet in his presence, to focus on him. To help us do that we need first of all to be in a relaxed and comfortable position so that we can give God our attention. To bring us into the presence of God we need to quieten our hearts and minds, to let go the things of the day around us, to breathe gently and rhythmically. Some people find it useful to read a verse or a short passage of the Bible and to allow their reflection on that to flow into prayer; others like to have an object (a lighted candle, perhaps) upon which to focus.

To give **shape** to your prayer, you may wish to use a simple form of the daily office (Morning or Evening Prayer) or to use the pattern of the acronym ACTS (Adoration, Confession, Thanksgiving, Supplication – the wonder of God, saying sorry, giving thanks, asking for things for others and ourselves). In all times of prayer there should be a time of quiet as we listen to God.

Formal prayers in church can sometimes make us feel that we have to use special sorts of **language** when we pray. We don't. Just be yourself and say things that are on your heart in your own way. God's not a liturgical snob! Some people find it helpful to have a book of prayers that they can draw from.

Others prefer only to use their own words. I guess most people do a mixture of both. What matters is what is right for you.

If all that has been said here makes it sound as though you can only pray if you have lots of time, don't forget that there is also value in those quick little **'arrow' prayers** that we offer amid the rush of the day which keep the lines of communication with God open.

As in other areas of life, it can be helpful to have someone to talk to about how you are finding prayer (and other aspects of your spiritual journey). Such people are variously referred to as spiritual directors, prayer partners or soul friends. They are someone you feel able to trust and to be honest with, and who will travel with you on your journey.

Group session three

Opening prayer

We are in your presence, God our Father.
You are with us, the Lord of all.
We come to learn: open us to your Spirit,
show us your way, teach us your truth.

Lord Jesus, you taught your disciples how to pray;
lead us by your Spirit as we learn to pray.
Help us to quieten our hearts and our minds,
that we may know your presence with us
and focus our thoughts on you,
that as we pray for others and for ourselves
we may do so in accordance with your will.
To you be the glory.
Amen.

Welcome

The leader introduces the session.

Activity

In pairs, share the object you have brought with you which has especial significance for you in your relationship with a friend or family member. Say what feelings the object arouses in you.

As a group, discuss what object might suggest a special significance for you in your relationship with God.

The leader sets out, so that everyone can see them, a candle, a cross (or crucifix) and an icon or picture of Jesus. Everyone is asked to sit quietly and to focus on these objects, each one in turn. A piece of suitable music might be played.

Then discuss together which, if any, of these objects helps you to focus your thoughts on God and in what way. Would anyone have chosen something else?

Reading

> [Jesus said,] 'Pray then in this way:
> Our Father in heaven,
> hallowed be your name.
> Your kingdom come.
> Your will be done,
> on earth as it is in heaven.
> Give us this day our daily bread.
> And forgive us our debts
> as we also have forgiven our debtors.
> And do not bring us to the time of trial,
> But rescue us from the evil one.
>
> *Matthew 6:9-13*

What does this prayer say about:

• Our relationship with God?

• The purposes of God?

• Our relationship with others?

• Our own needs?

Do you think this prayer omits any major aspect of prayer?

Input

There are, at least, two questions that are often asked when it comes to prayer:

• Does God always answer prayer?

• How does God answer prayer?

An answer to a request may be 'No'. A child might ask a parent to allow them to sleep out in the park for a night and the parent will tell them they can't. The 'No' is still an answer, even though it isn't the one the child wants. A good parent will be responding out of a concern for the child, not just to be negative. They may know that the park is closed at night, that there is going to be a storm that night, that the park is not a safe place to be after dark. God certainly does not give us everything we want. He knows better than we do what is for our good.

Books on prayer sometimes suggest that God always answers prayer: sometimes with 'Yes', sometimes with 'No' and sometimes with 'Not yet'. The critic says that since that covers all eventualities there is no difference between God answering prayer and events just working out with no reference to God.

God is sovereign over his creation and therefore we might think that he can do anything and everything. What we call miracles would seem to indicate this. Some people report amazing answers to prayer, when God has 'out of the blue' provided for them, healed them, protected them, guided them. But we also have to bear in mind:

- The way the universe works is the way God made it. If God constantly interfered with the laws of nature, there would be chaos.

- God has given us freedom that we are called to use responsibly, but we don't always, and we would never learn if every time we did something wrong he 'magically' put it right to get us out of a tight spot.

- In spite of prayer, people do go hungry, are unsafe, do die. What may be very important is how we respond to such events, which can feel very negative.

In pairs or as a group, discuss:

- Does God always answer prayer?

- How and in what ways does God answer prayer?

Reading

> [Jesus said,] 'Whenever you pray, do not be like the hypocrites; for they love to stand and pray in the synagogues and at the street corners, so that they may be seen by others. Truly I tell you, they have received their reward. But whenever you pray, go into your room and shut the door and pray to your Father who is in secret; and your Father who sees in secret will reward you.'
>
> *Matthew 6:5, 6*

Jesus had quite a lot to say about not 'showing off' spiritually – either in prayers or in giving to charity. But here we take note of the private nature of prayer and how we go about that.

The leader encourages the group to:

a. Sit comfortably, but not lounging. The weight of the body should run through the spine without straining the back.

b. Starting at the top of the head, consciously relax the muscles right down to the toes. Hold your hands loosely in your lap.

c. Breathe evenly and slowly.

d. Either focus on an object already identified (candle, cross, picture) or close your eyes. Focus attention on God and allow other thoughts to drift away.

e. Spend five minutes silently in prayer.

The group may find it helpful if some suitable music is played quietly – but this will need to be agreed upon beforehand.

The group may wish to discuss, in pairs and then all together, how that felt.

Activity

Decide together on a major item of concern that is current in the news (such as a war, a famine, a natural disaster, a report on child abuse), then discuss:

• What are the issues?

• Who should be prayed for?

• What should be prayed for?

• What might be done as well as prayer?

Reflection

> Likewise the Spirit helps us in our weakness; for we do not know how to pray as we ought, but that very Spirit intercedes with sighs too deep for words. And God, who searches the heart, knows what is the mind of the Spirit, because the Spirit intercedes for the saints according to the will of God.
>
> *Romans 8:26, 27*

Holy Spirit, will you be
one who intercedes for me?
When I wonder what to pray
how to phrase the words I say.
Come in might and majesty –
help me in my frailty.

Holy Spirit, will you be
one who intercedes for me?
When I lack the words to tell
what my feelings say too well
speak through every sigh and groan
making my emotions known.

Holy Spirit, will you be
one who intercedes for me?
Come, and search my heart and mind,
my desires and motives find;
take my deepest thoughts and cares,
turn them into fervent prayers.

Holy Spirit, will you be
one who intercedes for me?
You alone can understand
what the mind of God has planned –
and within his will you lead
all for whom you intercede.

Martin E. Leckebusch (b. 1962)

Prayer is not just what we do; it is also what God does in us, through his Spirit.

Prayer

Almighty God,
you are Lord of all and worthy of all praise.
Teach us how to pray
and guide us by your Spirit,
that all our words and thoughts
may be directed to your will
and to the glory of your name.
Forgive us our self-centredness,
but give us a concern of others
and a love for you,
in Jesus' name.
Amen.

The next session

Look in the news (TV, radio or newspapers) for a 'good' story and a 'bad' story which you can share with the group next time. They could be about wonderful things or disasters in nature, or stories which reveal the good and bad aspects of men and women.

The world

Introduction – you will find it helpful to read this before the group session

Religion, it is sometimes said, is there to ask the Big Questions. A recent poster campaign in London by the Humanist Society, 'Thought for a commute', was also focused around a Big Question: 'What's it all for?' The 'all' presumably refers to human life, creation, the universe and everything, and the question implies that there is some sort of purpose to it all. A Christian's description of what that purpose is would, of course, differ considerably from that offered by a humanist. The Christian doesn't believe that this world and all the created order simply came about by chance, even if it was as the result of a Big Bang.

Scientists can give us some idea of **how** the universe came into existence, and even though their theories change or get modified there is no reason simply to dismiss them. Science has the techniques to investigate such a question. But it is less able to give answers to **why** the universe came into existence. The Christian answer is that God wanted it that way – he willed it, created it and has a purpose for it. That is a faith statement, not a scientific one, but it is not irrational and should not simply be dismissed because of that.

The alternative for a Christian does not have to be a choice between science and Genesis, although there are some Christians who do accept the biblical account as a literal description of the origins of the universe. Others accept that the story of creation in Genesis is not intended to be a scientific description of what happened but is rather a story that shows the beginning of the relationship between God and his creation, especially that with human beings. It has even been suggested that the account was actually in the form of a song. Now, that's an interesting idea.

The Hebrew understanding of creation is all about the creation of **order out of chaos** (it is not about creation from nothing – that's a 'modern' idea). To that extent it reflects what the scientific view says about 'laws of nature'. God's world is intended to be an orderly world. Its ways are dynamic but not chaotic. Given the same conditions, water will boil tomorrow at the same temperature as it did today. And such orderliness is, says the Bible, good. 'God saw everything that he had made, and indeed, it was very good' (Genesis 1:31). There is so much that is wonderful about the created order – it has beauty and amazing diversity; it can be awesome and majestic, subtle and benevolent. But not always, not everywhere, not for everyone.

The world can also be a terrifying place – a place of pain and destruction, a place of disease and disaster. Nature can be **wonderful but it can also be cruel**. Relationships can be loving but they can also be abusive. Human beings can be amazing but they can also be terrifying. In the so-called story of the Fall, Genesis seeks to give an account as to why this should be so. And humanity bears the responsibility. The good order of creation gives way to the possibility of disorder, and order will only be restored when there is a new heaven and a new earth (a new creation). There is not only wrong in the individual human heart (sin), but there are also wrongs in families, communities and nations, and there are wrongs globally. There is not harmony in our relations with one another nor with our environment. In other words, it is a good world in which things go wrong – there is good and evil, right and wrong.

We need to be a little careful how we use these terms. We talk about 'bad' weather, but it is actually only 'bad' from our perspective, not in itself. To a farmer longing for rain, another dry, sunny day is bad weather, but to the holidaymaker, rain would be bad. Many natural disasters are merely the result of the natural world working out the way it has been ordered – they are seen as disasters because of their effect upon us. A volcano is fine, even dramatically awesome, if it erupts and no one is hurt. Its lava replenishes the earth's natural resources of minerals. But if its ash covers hikers walking on its slopes (as happened in Japan in September 2014), then it is a disaster. Should we pray to God to keep us from such disasters? Is it right to expect him to interfere in the way he has ordered the physical world if it keeps people from being hurt?

Of course, some disasters occur because of human action – think of global warming, or of flooding in towns where houses are built on flood plains. So we should ask God to help us to be more responsible in our actions, to make us good stewards of the good world he has given us, to enable us to strive for reconciliation when relationships are broken, and for peace when there is violence. But it is so easy to get things wrong.

In fact, it feels as though we are almost programmed to make mistakes. None of us is perfect. It's as though there is **a bias to the wrong**. Scientists have suggested that this is merely the way we have developed. It's in our genes to be aggressive, selfish and competitive – humanity wouldn't have survived without such traits. But we are also sociable, caring and gentle. So it's not all wrong. The tension between right and wrong is a spiritual matter as well as a biological and moral one. How we deal with that tension is part of our spiritual journey, the way we grow towards greater spiritual maturity. It takes honesty, courage and humility – and a considerable degree of self-awareness and reliance on the grace of God. It's not even just a matter of willpower. As St Paul said, 'I can will what is right, but I cannot do it. For I do not do the good I want, but the evil I do not want is what I do' (Romans 7:18, 19).

Many, if not all, religions seek to give an explanation for this ambiguity in our world and in ourselves. They offer ways to combat the evil and to encourage the good. The Christian faith is very realistic about what is wrong, but it also offers supreme hope in the promise of forgiveness and the restoration of order in our relations with one another, with the world and with God. That is what salvation is about, demonstrated and made effective in God's outpouring of himself in Christ. Christ's death shows the lengths to which God goes to restore harmony and to bring salvation. He makes himself utterly vulnerable, putting himself in our hands, as it were, and loving us even when we utterly reject him. That is the way of God. That is the way of the cross. And the resurrection is the 'proof' that his way prevails. Love conquers all!

Is God still active in his world? Most Christians would want to answer that with a Yes. They do not hold to the idea that God created the world and then just went away and left it to its own devices. The differences of opinion occur around the way we understand how God acts in the world. It has often been claimed that when we don't understand how things work we say God does it. There is a gap in our knowledge and we fill the gap with God. But that merely squeezes God into a smaller and smaller area as our knowledge increases. So the eruption of a volcano with tragic results for those living nearby was seen, before there was an understanding of the geophysical forces at work, as the work of an angry god. Religious rituals were created to appease the anger of such a god. The Hebrew religion saw such events as the work of a righteous, not an arbitrary, God who was responding to the moral and religious faithlessness of his people. Righteous behaviour resulted in God giving good results – plentiful harvests, fertile flocks. And there are many who still see events and God's actions in this way. Others are less happy with a view of God who manipulates the order of his creation. They see God's action through his presence in the very processes of the created order and in the responsible or irresponsible actions of human beings who 'steward' God's creation.

So what about **miracles**? Plenty of people bear witness to the fact that miracles, especially of healing, still occur and that God has healed where medical science failed. Such healings are seen to be God's answer to prayer, and that when there is no healing, God is understood to have a different but still loving plan for that person. Some Christians would say that our prayers are one way in which we seek to bring our lives, our intentions and our concerns in line with the loving purposes of God. When, as it were, our concerns and God's concerns coincide, line up, then the creative power of God, always present in creation, is able to do amazing things.

Some events that were reported as miracles in the Bible may have more 'natural' explanations these days. Some healings may be understood in psychosomatic terms. Some events in nature may have been perfectly natural but simply misunderstood or interpreted in terms of divine action, such as an eclipse. We sometimes forget just how much our normal way of thinking about things has undergone huge changes since the Renaissance, even among devout Christians. It is also noticeable that in his Gospel, John does not talk about miracles but about signs – events that demonstrated truths about God or about Jesus. To John, these truths were more significant than the events themselves.

But after all is said and done, one event remains central to the Christian gospel which, on any reading, is a miraculous event. And that is the resurrection. Through it, all that Jesus had said and done was vindicated by God's action of raising him from death. It showed that the way of risky and vulnerable love was God's way. It showed that God has the final say, even over death. It showed that God's way of reconciling humanity to himself through Christ had been achieved. The cross showed just how costly that way is. Christ's resurrection gives immense hope and comfort to countless people who find in it the promise that there is more to life than the time we spend on earth.

None of the approaches suggested here is a quick or easy solution to what can puzzle us about the way the world is and how we understand God's action in it. Our own answers may change over time in the light of our growing faith and ongoing experience, but it would be very difficult to make sense of the Bible or of the Christian faith through the ages if there were not some way of believing that this is God's world that he cares about and is involved in.

Group session four

Opening prayer

We are in your presence, God our Father.
You are with us, the Lord of all.
We come to learn: open us to your Spirit,
show us your way, teach us your truth.

Almighty God, this is your world,
full of beauty and wonder,
a created order that is both amazing and terrifying,
a world that delights us and puzzles us.
Help us to see your activity in your world
and to bear the stewardship of it
with responsibility and care.
We ask this in Jesus' name.
Amen.

Welcome

The leader introduces the session.

Activity

In pairs or threes, share the newspaper stories you have brought with you – looking first at the 'good' stories and then the 'bad'. What do they say about our world and about human beings? How do you feel when you hear such stories?

Share your general findings as a whole group.

Input

The poet Gerard Manley Hopkins wrote, 'The world is charged with the grandeur of God'. In 'In Memoriam', Lord Tennyson suggested that nature is 'red in tooth and claw'.

The estimated deaths from floods in China in 1931 ranged from one million to four million. An earthquake and tsunami in the Indian Ocean in 2004 is estimated to have killed more than one quarter of a million people. Around 200,000 people are said to have died in an avalanche in Peru in 1970.

If this is God's world, why do such things happen? Could he not stop them? Do we choose to see God only in the wonder of nature?

In September 2014 Alan Henning, a taxi driver from Manchester, was beheaded by the so-called Islamic State. The outrage reverberated around the world and the event was condemned by many Muslim as well as Western leaders. Alan had gone to Syria to help bring aid and support to people who were suffering as a result of the war in that country. His altruism and sacrifice were celebrated and applauded. One commentator said that the example of this one man was more powerful than all the guns of the terrorists, and it would be his legacy that would be remembered. An ISIS spokesman said that they would not cease until the infidels of the West had been destroyed. They would prevail.

Activity

How do you view these contrasting comments?

Together, consider how faith affects your view of both what is 'good' and what is 'bad'.

Reading

> I do not understand my own actions. For I do not do what I want, but I do the very thing I hate. Now if I do what I do not want, I agree that the law is good. But in fact it is no longer I that do it, but sin that dwells within me. For I know that nothing good dwells within me, that is, in my flesh. I can will

what is right, but I cannot do it. For I do not do the good I want, but the evil I do not want is what I do. Now if I do what I do not want, it is no longer I that do it, but sin that dwells within me.

Romans 7:15-20

There is therefore now no condemnation for those who are in Christ Jesus.

Romans 8:1

Reflect

Spend five minutes reflecting on your own life over the last week in the light of these readings. At the end of the five minutes, all say together:

Lord have mercy.
Christ have mercy.
Lord have mercy.

Activity

As a group, consider what action your church might undertake to tackle one local issue that affects people's quality of life. It might be environmental; it could concern loneliness; it could be for the young, for the elderly or for lone parents; or perhaps it might be an improvement in bus services.

If the action were to include prayer asking for God's help, what help might that include and how would you expect God to answer your prayer?

Reflection

Longing for light, we wait in darkness.
Longing for truth, we turn to you.
Make us your own, your holy people,
light for the world to see.

Christ be our light! Shine in our hearts.
Shine through the darkness, Christ, be our light!
Shine in your church gathered today.

Longing for peace, our world is troubled.
Longing for hope, many despair.
Your word alone has power to save us.
Make us your living voice.

Longing for food, many are hungry.
Longing for water, many still thirst.
Make us your bread, broken for others,
shared until all are fed.

Longing for shelter, many are homeless.
Longing for warmth, many are cold.
Make us your building, sheltering others,
walls made of living stone.

Many the gifts, many the people,
many the hearts that yearn to belong.
Let us be servants to one another,
making your kingdom come.

Bernadette Farrell (b. 1957)

Prayer

Fill us, Lord, with your hope,
that the anxieties of the world may not overcome us.
Fill us, Lord, with your love,
that the fears of the world may not defeat us.
Give us a vision of your possibilities
for the world and for all people,
that we may know your presence with us,
and fulfil our responsibilities as your servants.
In Jesus' name we ask this.
Amen.

Session five

God

Introduction – you will find it helpful to read this before the group session

'Oh, my God!' exclaimed the teenager as she saw her GCSE results. She was delighted. Her results were better than she had expected.

When she asked her boyfriend what his results were like, he replied, 'God awful,' and then quickly added, 'Only kidding.'

In spite of the second commandment, the name of God is constantly taken 'in vain'. If those youngsters were asked who or what the god they were addressing was like, the chances are they would have little or no idea. They might not even be 'bovvered'. And youngsters wouldn't be the only ones.

Human beings have, as far as we can tell, always called on gods – for help, to ensure good hunting and good crops, in times of war, in celebrations, in birth and in death. Religious ritual is as old as the hills. Belief in gods goes back to prehistoric times – gods of lightning, gods of thunder, gods of fertility, gods of war. There were big gods and little gods, local gods, personal gods. Many peoples believed in a whole number of gods – one for every occasion. Jews, Christians and Muslims believe there is only one God.

Even when there was a close identification with a physical object – a tree, a mountain or a river, for example – the god was most often understood to inhabit the object rather than actually being the object. The gods have always had something of a mystery about them, elusive to full description or knowledge. And although Christians believe God to be a God who reveals himself (in nature, in the Bible, through Jesus), nevertheless he remains a mystery. The Bible says no one has ever seen God, although in Jesus we do see God in human terms. God is spirit, we say, and spirit is by its nature intangible, not readily contained or explained.

When Moses asked God who he was, what his name was, all God gave him was a puzzle – 'I am who I am' (Exodus 3:13, 14). If we want to try and describe God we have to resort to imagery, to symbols, to pictures, to music and even a combination of all of them. It is important to remember this – **all** our language about God is an approximation. When we say God is 'He', when we look at representations of God that show him as an old man (in the Sistine Chapel, for example), this is an imaginative likeness. The idea of God being male arose in a patriarchal society. But Isaiah, for example, also described God in female terms (Isaiah 66:13), and so did Mother Julian of Norwich. Modern feminists frequently do so as well, not to be annoying but to make the point that it can be as right to call God Mother as it is to call God Father. God does not have a physical gender.

Cynics take the Christian idea that God made human beings in his image and turn it on its head, saying that people of faith merely make God in their own image. Before we rush to protest against such a slur, we should recognise that there is actually some truth in this. Our descriptions of what God is like, how he behaves, the sort of interaction he has with us and the world, do reflect human experience and inevitably depend on human language or symbols. Even when we assert that it is not simply a matter of our imaginations and projections, that God has revealed himself – through nature, through messages, through dreams, through Jesus – we have to admit that it is through human forms of communication, especially words, that we express what God has revealed. We may well then want to go on to say that the way those words are used take us beyond our human experience to an insight into the Divine. Thus, to say that God is love (perhaps the most fundamental statement that can be made by a Christian about God) certainly begins with our understanding of human love at its best, but in the light of Jesus' life, death and resurrection it goes beyond that.

While God has always been God, human understanding of God has not always been the same – not even within the Jewish/Christian tradition. Our understanding of God does change. In the early days of the Hebrews he was a tribal God, a god of war. There is also evidence that he was understood at one time to be part of a whole heavenly court of divine beings. Among all the gods, the Hebrews came to understand that Yahweh was 'their' God, and that he was the only one to whom they should give their allegiance. Only later did they reach the conclusion that there was in fact only one God.

People sometimes suggest that the God of the Old Testament is a very different God from that of the New. In the Old Testament, it is said, he is a God of vengeance and punishment, while in the New Testament he is a God of forgiveness and mercy, offering us salvation. Whereas in the Old Testament he is the God of the Hebrews (the Jews), in the New Testament he is the God of all people. This is, at best, a rather crude analysis, but there is some truth in it – not because God changed but because human perception of God changed in changing circumstances. We might note, for example, that Jesus' mission was almost exclusively to the Jews, but as the mission of the Church spread it included the Gentile world, and people's views of what God required of his followers also altered. But we should expect this of a God who is dynamic and full of surprises.

Our own experience and understanding of God can also change. It is unlikely that the way you view God now is exactly the same as the way you thought about him (if, in fact, you did) when you were younger. As you grow in the faith, you may well find that you view God differently, speak about him differently and pray to him differently.

A personal understanding of God is very important. It is what faith and trust in God involves. And that understanding will always be partly shaped by our personal circumstances and experiences, our personality and our make-up. Our way of talking about God will to that extent be 'our' way. But that does not mean we can just say anything we like about God and claim it as the truth – not even if we add, 'That is the truth for me.' God's revealing of himself through nature, through the Bible and especially through Jesus means that we do not start just from ourselves and only have our own ideas and experience. We draw upon the whole range of Jewish and Christian insight from across the ages. We have the authority of the Bible, we have the authority of the Church, we have the authority of tradition. The Creeds offer us a summary of what the Christian Church believes about God. They, of course, reflect terminology from the time they were written, influenced by Greek philosophical ideas, but they have stood the test of time and provide a basic benchmark for us.

The Christian faith has as its central belief about God the understanding that God is all about relationships, built on and flowing from love. God is love. There is love in God flowing between the Father, Son and Holy Spirit. Love flows from God out into creation and to humanity. And God has made us so that we can choose to enter into this relationship of love and love God back and share God's love for his creation and for other people. And love is, in the end, a wonderful and glorious mystery.

Group session five

Opening prayer

We are in your presence, God our Father.
You are with us, the Lord of all.
We come to learn: open us to your Spirit,
show us your way, teach us your truth.

You are the only God, mystery beyond mystery,
whose love embraces us and holds us.
Help us to know you more fully –
through the words of Scripture,
through the story of Jesus,
through your Spirit within us.
Amen.

Welcome

The leader introduces the session.

Activity

In threes, discuss how each of you came to know God. What has been most influential in helping you to grow in your knowledge of God?

As a group, using a large piece of paper (perhaps a flip chart), write up as many brief descriptions or titles of God that you can. Choose a few of them and ask these questions of them:

- From what context did the title/description arise? For example, 'King' arose from the experience of monarchy.

- Does the title or description have any special meaning when associated with God? For example, 'Father' – not physically; of all people.

- Are there any titles that have largely lost their meaning these days?

Each person might be asked which title/description means most to them and why.

Reading

> In the year that King Uzziah died, I saw the Lord sitting on a throne, high and lofty; and the hem of his robe filled the temple. Seraphs were in attendance above him; each had six wings: with two they covered their faces, and with two they covered their feet, and with two they flew. And one called to another and said:
> 'Holy, holy, holy is the Lord of hosts;
> The whole earth is full of his glory.'
>
> *Isaiah 6:1-3*

Discuss how you might understand this vision of God. What was the prophet doing when he had this vision? Where was he? What was the political/social context of the time? What does it tell you about God?

What other biblical passages help you to gain a picture of God?

Input

The belief that God is Trinity (three persons and one God) is fundamental and distinctive to Christianity. It highlights a number of things about God:

- The mystery of God
- The uniqueness of God
- The being of God as relationship
- The interwoven but different ways we experience God.

It is not a puzzle to solve but a mystery to enter into and explore. In seeking to understand what is a theological image rather than a mathematical formula, people have used other images – the lover, the beloved and the love they share (Augustine); the book in the mind of the author, the book as object, the book in the mind of the reader (Dorothy Sayers). At its heart it emphasises that God is love: love that exists between the persons of the Trinity, love that flows out from God in creation, love that God shows in his care of humanity. The fact that it is called 'Holy' emphasises the special, divine nature of this Trinity (as opposed to the Suffolk Trinity, for example, which is the Suffolk Punch Horse, Red Pole Cattle and Black-faced Sheep).

Activity

Each person is asked to draw or describe how they 'see' the Trinity.

Reflection

God is love: let heaven adore him;
God is love: let earth rejoice;
let creation sing before him,
and exalt him with one voice.
He who laid the earth's foundation,
he who spread the heavens above,
he who breathes through all creation,
he is love, eternal love.

God is love: and he enfoldeth
all the world in one embrace;
with unfailing grasp he holdeth
every child of every race.
And when human hearts are breaking
under sorrow's iron rod,
then they find the self-same aching
deep within the heart of God.

God is love: and though with blindness
sin afflicts the human soul,
God's eternal loving-kindness
guides and heals and makes us whole.
Sin and death and hell shall never
o'er us final triumph gain;
God is love, so love for ever
o'er the universe must reign.

Timothy Rees (1874–1939)

Prayer

God of love,
help us to be more loving;
help us to love you more fully
and to be more loving to our neighbours.
In the name of the Father who loves us in creating,
and of the Son who loves us in his dying,
and of the Spirit who loves us in her guiding,
one God, one love.
Amen.

Session six

God: Father, Son and Holy Spirit

Introduction – you will find it helpful to read this before the group session

Artists have never found it particularly easy to represent the Trinity. There's usually a venerable old man with a beard for the Father, a young man for the Son and, hovering around somewhere, a white dove for the Holy Spirit. More mysterious and less obvious is the famous icon by Rublev with its reference to the Abraham story at the oaks of Mamre (Genesis 18). As we noted in the previous session, all language and imagery that seeks to express our understanding of God is in the end an imaginative approximation – the best we can do from a human standpoint guided by divine revelation. It is that human standpoint which usually makes it easiest for us (as for artists) to think of the Father and the Son and less easy to convey what we mean by the Holy Spirit.

When we use the term **Father** about God we are saying that God is 'fatherlike'. In the Lord's Prayer (Matthew 6:9-13), Jesus taught his disciples to address God as 'Our Father' – the implication being that he is father of all, not just my father. By adding 'in heaven', he was clearly indicating that there is something special about this father. He is like but not exactly the same as earthly fathers.

Jesus himself addressed God as *Abba* (Father), although the experts differ as to whether this was equivalent to the term 'daddy', such as a child would use. Either way, it indicates an intimate, personal relationship. God is not an inanimate, impersonal force like fate or destiny. Nor is he arbitrary and cruel in the way Gloucester in *King Lear* suggests when he states: 'As flies to wanton boys are we to the gods.'[4]

---

4. William Shakespeare, King Lear, Act 4, Scene 1.

The Hebrew religion had clearly developed an under-standing of God that brought together mercy and judgement, righteousness and morality. God could be stern but was also compassionate. He set out boundaries for behaviour and expected them to be honoured. He had authority, emphasised by other titles such as 'King' and 'Lord'. In Christ we see him risking what was most precious to him (his Son) for the sake of restoring humanity's relationship with himself. A reconciling, forgiving, welcoming, saving Father who loves his creation (compare with the father in the story of the prodigal son – Luke 15:11-32).

'Father' also implies the creation of a family, and God the Father is normally closely associated with the creation of all that exists. Unlike some of the religions around them, the Hebrew religion did not have a sexual notion of this creative act (consider the Baalistic use of temple prostitutes). Indeed, in the Genesis story, man is a piece of creative art moulded from the earth, while the created universe is brought about by command – God speaks and it is so.

We need to remember this when we speak of God as Father to the **Son** who is Jesus, not least because in the Creeds Jesus is identified as the only begotten Son of the Father, indicating his unique relationship with God but using a term associated with physical fathering. In the Bible, a number of people are identified as sons of God. It is a term often used about the king, for example. It implies a close relationship with God, who invests the king with both honour and responsibility, and in some sense identifying the king as God's representative. It would therefore be quite possible to call Jesus God's son, without necessarily implying that he was divine. Indeed, it remains a matter of discussion among scholars as to how far Jesus, while on earth, was understood to be God. Some argue that this developed after the resurrection and, in part at least, through the writings of people like St Paul and St John the Evangelist. The belief soon established itself, however, and the discussion moved from whether or not Jesus was God to how people could understand that he was both God and man. And it was the Creeds as we have them now that set out the Church's way of answering that.

The Gospels of Matthew and Luke provide telling accounts of the birth of the baby Jesus. Together they build up the picture of the special nature of this child, not least in the way he was conceived – through the power of the Holy Spirit, according to Luke (Luke 1:34, 35). Together with the accounts of his life, and not least through the way in which his miraculous powers are described, it is not too difficult for us to come to some understanding of Jesus as God.

So did Jesus always exist – eternally exist – in heaven before his birth? This is more difficult to grasp, and St John has his own way of expressing this. He uses the idea of the Word of God – God's self-expression. He says that it always existed and that it was this divine Word that became flesh and dwelt among us (John 1:14). This is what we mean by incarnation – 'enfleshment'.

The importance of believing that Jesus is the Son of God – that he *is* God – is paramount when we consider what Jesus is understood to have achieved through the cross. His self-giving, self-sacrificing love showed the saving activity of God. It was through Jesus that the great rift between humanity and God, caused by sin, was bridged. And only God could do that. Jesus, the Son of God, was saving the world.

This is what faith believes. It is not about what can be proved, and all our attempts to speak about it are less than perfect. The divine–human nature of Jesus and his saving work is ultimately a mystery. We enter into it and know our relationship with God is one of love and acceptance. We share the good news that this is available for all people and, even though our words can be powerful and persuasive, we know they will never fully capture the fullness of God the Father and his Son.

And this is equally true when we come to God the **Holy Spirit**. For Spirit speaks of the very nature of God ('God is spirit, and those who worship him must worship him in spirit and truth.' John 4:23). The Spirit is associated with the activity of God – in creation, in the work of the prophets, in the incarnation, at the baptism of Jesus, in the commissioning of the disciples (John 20:22, 23; Acts 2:1-4) and in the guidance of the mission of the Church (Acts 16:6). The Holy Spirit sustains and enables, inspires and empowers. It is through the work of God the Holy Spirit that people have the gifts that are needed for the building-up of the people of God, the Church (see 1 Corinthians 12) – gifts of prophecy and teaching, of leadership and healing.

Exactly how the persons of the Trinity relate is, of course, part of the mystery of God. The Creeds make it quite clear that each person is distinct, yet each is also God. Here is one attempt to try and picture the relationship:

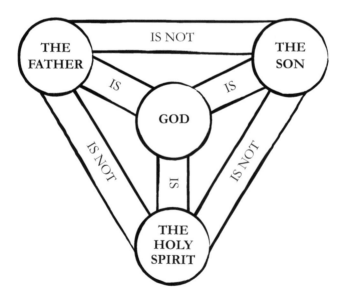

The Shack by William P. Young[5] is an attempt to explore the Trinity through a fictional story.

At key points in people's lives, the Church asks specifically for the gift of the Holy Spirit to guide and strengthen them. The baptism service speaks of being daily renewed by God's anointing Spirit; in the water of baptism we are reborn and offered new life by the power of the Spirit; it is through the one Spirit we are all baptised into one body. In the confirmation service the opening prayer asks God to 'guide and strengthen us by the Spirit', and the bishop asks that the Holy Spirit may rest upon the candidates. It is by the power of the Holy Spirit that in the Holy Communion service the gifts of bread and wine become for us the body and blood of Christ. In a marriage service the priest prays 'that the Holy Spirit will guide and strengthen the couple'. At an ordination service the bishop lays hands on the candidate and prays, 'Send down the Holy Spirit on your servant N for the office and work of a deacon/priest/bishop in your Church.'

It is the full being and work of God that is called upon when a priest blesses people in the name of God the Father, Son and Holy Spirit.

---

5. Hodder and Stoughton, 2008.

Group session six

Opening prayer

We are in your presence, God our Father.
You are with us, the Lord of all.
We come to learn; open us to your Spirit,
show us your way, teach us your truth.

Creator Father, you have made us,
and we delight in you.

Saviour Son, we give you thanks,
that through you we are reconciled to God.

Holy Spirit, inspire us and strengthen us,
that we may live lives that are pleasing to God.

Amen.

Welcome

The leader introduces the session.

Activity

A primary school pupil was recently asked the difference between the persons of the Trinity. She replied, 'Jesus wears sandals and the others don't.'

- How do you distinguish between the Father, Son and Holy Spirit?

- What are the significant roles that you believe each of them has?

Input

The person of the Trinity to whom we most often pray may well be more determined by our life experiences and how we imagine things than by our theology. A child who has never known a father may either find it very hard to picture God as Father or have always prayed to God as the Father he/she never had.

In a prep school in Kent, a very large and rather gruesome crucifix hung on the stairs going up to the boys' dormitory. Some of the boys found it quite frightening, and it made praying to Jesus difficult. Other people find the humanity of Jesus makes him much more accessible than either the Father or the Holy Spirit.

The use of the old-fashioned term 'Holy Ghost' has obviously given some people a very strange perception of God as Holy Spirit and disinclined them to address the Holy Spirit in prayer.

Some people only ever pray to God – without distinguishing between the persons.

Activity

Who do you most often pray to – Father, Son or Holy Spirit? Discuss this in pairs or threes. It might tell you quite a lot about how you view God.

Times of intercession are sometimes introduced with these words: 'In the power of the Spirit and in union with Christ, let us pray to the Father.' In what ways does this help you to see prayer as involving all the persons of the Trinity?

Reading

There are few direct references to the Trinity in the New Testament, but this occurs at the end of St Matthew's Gospel:

> And Jesus came and said to them, 'All authority
> in heaven and earth has been given to me. Go
> therefore and make disciples of all nations,

> baptizing them in the name of the Father and of
> the Son and of the Holy Spirit, and teaching them
> to obey everything that I have commanded you.
> And remember, I am with you always, to the end
> of the age.
>
> *Matthew 28:18-20*

This may well reflect the early Church's practice of baptising converts in the name of the Trinity.

In his Gospel, St John gives us an extended passage of sayings by Jesus at the Last Supper. It includes this, which relates all three persons of the Trinity:

> I have said these things to you while I am still
> with you. But the Advocate, the Holy Spirit, whom
> the Father will send in my name, will teach you
> everything, and remind you of all that I have said
> to you.
>
> *John 14:25, 26*

In his greetings at the beginning of his Letters, Paul never refers to the Holy Spirit. A typical greeting is:

> Grace to you and peace from God our Father and
> the Lord Jesus Christ.
>
> *Romans 1:7; 1 Corinthians 1:3; 2 Corinthians 1:2*

or

> Grace, mercy and peace from God the Father and
> Christ Jesus our Lord.
>
> *1 Timothy 1:2; 2 Timothy 1:2*

These may well have been common greetings among early Christians.

At the beginning of the Letter to the Galatians there is a more extended greeting which relates Jesus' self-sacrifice to the saving purpose of the Father:

> Grace to you and peace from God our Father and the Lord Jesus Christ, who gave himself for our sins to set us free from the present evil age, according to the will of our God and Father, to whom be the glory for ever and ever. Amen.
>
> *Galatians 1:3-5*

Activity

As a group, suggest some greetings or some blessings that make reference to all three persons of the Holy Trinity.

Reflection

Father, Lord of all creation,
ground of Being, Life and Love;
height and depth beyond description,
only life in you can prove:
you are mortal life's dependence:
thought, speech, sight are ours by grace;
yours is every hour's existence,
sovereign Lord of time and space.

Jesus Christ, the Man for Others,
we, your people, make our prayer:
help us love – as sisters, brothers –
all whose burdens we can share.
Where your name binds us together,
you, Lord Christ, will surely be;
where no selfishness can sever
there your love the world may see.

Holy Spirit, rushing, burning
wind and flame of Pentecost,
fire our hearts afresh with yearning
to regain what we have lost.
May your love unite our action,
never more to speak alone:
God in us abolish faction,
God, through us your love make known.

Stewart Cross (1928–1989)

Prayer

Father God, creator and protector,
bless us on our way.
Son of God, saviour and friend,
bless us on our way.
Holy Spirit, guide and comforter,
bless us on our way.
Amen.

Session seven

Growing on

Introduction – you will find it helpful to read this before the group session

In the notes to the initiation services of *Common Worship*, and in the section on confirmation on the Church of England website,[6] confirmation is seen as part of a process of initiation into membership of the Church, the body of Christ, that is founded on baptism.

The significance of baptism lies not only in the fact that Jesus was himself baptised but that he also commanded that those who were led to follow him should be baptised in his name. In baptism a person is, through God's grace and through having declared their personal trust in God, made a member of the community of faith (the Church). The person is granted the gift of the Holy Spirit to strengthen and guide their life, and is drawn into the life of the Holy Trinity.

Baptism is not only a significant personal moment for the individual but is also a 'community' event. It is significant in the life of the Church locally and universally. Confirmation is a further step in a person's commitment of faith and witness and service. In the words of the much-used, and sometimes overused, phrase, this is all part of a journey. But it is also part of a process of growing – personally, spiritually, in the fellowship of others and in one's relationship with God. It is a start, not a completion.

There is an often-heard joke concerning the problem of bats in churches: if only we could confirm them we would never see them again! Sadly, too often, and especially with teenagers, confirmation has been considered a rite to go through and then,

6. https://www.churchofengland.org/our-faith/confirmation.aspx
(accessed 15 December 2014).

having done it, one can go off and forget the Church. That is not how it is intended to be. But if we are to journey on positively, if we are to grow as disciples of Jesus, maturing into the full stature of Christ (Ephesians 4:13), then we shall have to put in some effort – have a regular diet, exercise, learn, be active and look after ourselves.

Regular diet

We know that we won't grow or stay healthy if we don't eat properly and regularly. What is true of our physical well-being is also true of our spiritual well-being. We need regular nourishment – through our reading and study of the Bible, through prayer and worship, through fellowship with others.

As we have already seen, **the Bible** is a wonderful but quite complex book. Through it God can speak to us amid the changing events in our lives and as we grow and develop in faith. It rewards regular and careful reading, and books and Bible study notes can be helpful. You might feel like reading the Bible straight through, just as it is, allowing the Spirit to take the word and speak through it. For others there are any number of different ways of dividing the Bible up – by using a lectionary of daily readings, or concentrating on the Sunday's readings throughout the week, for example. For it to become the word of God for you, and not merely a series of words, you will need to take a bit of time not only to read the passage but also to reflect upon it, seeing what it says to you in your particular circumstances at this time, what it says about God, what it says about the world.

We need also **to pray and to worship**, for as we have seen, these are the routes for building up our relationship with God, for listening to him, for sharing our lives and concerns with him, our celebrations and our confessions. And we benefit by doing this both in the privacy of our own space and in the fellowship of others, joining in and with the prayer of the Church.

Exercise

Doctors and experts keep telling us that exercise is vital for health. But what does that mean for the spirit? It means, among other things, exercising the gifts that we have been given. The author of the Letter to Ephesians saw individual growth to maturity as the result of everyone using the gifts they were given – for the building-up of the body of Christ.

We have a part to play in the life of the Church – everyone does. And the Church is poorer and less healthy if we do not do that. It may take time to discern what our gifts are. Others may need to help us to see what God is calling us to do. It may be something 'up front' or something much more in the background – both are valuable. You have something to contribute – believe it.

Learn

No confirmation course can teach you all you need to know to be a mature disciple. Just as school should be the foundation of a lifetime of learning, not a dead-end, so, too, this course will have failed if it does not stir a desire in you to learn and carry on learning about God, about the way of Christ, and about what it means to be a disciple amid all the pressures and changes of modern life. As a student teacher I was taught that education was about 'learning for living'. That's what studying our faith is all about – not to become an academic theologian (although they have their place), but to grow in the art of living in Christ's way, making connections between our faith and our world.

Be active

The disciples of Jesus have a job to do – to look outward and to witness to others. For a few that could mean going out to the marketplace, to the shopping mall and proclaiming the gospel. But that's not the only or the most usual way to witness.

It may not even start with words – actions are often more telling. Noticing where help is needed and doing it and then being ready to say what has motivated you, what it is that spurs you on in terms of your faith: that is witness. It may be done quite quietly. You may feel hesitant about it. But don't fail to take the opportunities you do have. As you grow in confidence you will find that you don't simply wait for the opportunities – you make the opportunities.

Be active in caring, in the pursuit of truth and of justice – be a person who lives the values of the kingdom – love, peace, joy, generosity, justice, goodness, mercy, forgiveness. Lives lived according to these values are themselves a witness to the gospel.

Look after yourself

Does that sound selfish? It isn't. It's vital. And the most important way of looking after yourself is to draw upon the love and the presence of God who looks after you. Never lose belief in the fact that you are worth everything to God. Grow in the faith God has in you and you will grow in faith in God. Let the love of God fill you with a proper love for yourself – because only then will you grow in your love for others.

Our growing in our faith and in our discipleship does not depend entirely on us, although we do have our part to play. Growth is made possible because we draw upon the goodness of God and the love and care of others, so that we can grow in love of God and love of our neighbour, which is the fulfilling of the law and the mark of maturity.

Don't strive too hard. Give yourself space – time to reflect, time just to be. The quality time you give to others will be all the better for it.

And now, at the end of the course or after your confirmation, you might like to spend some time reflecting upon the ways in which this time of preparation and the confirmation have changed you.

Group session seven

Opening prayer

We are in your presence, God our Father.
You are with us, the Lord of all.
We come to learn: open us to your Spirit,
show us your way, teach us your truth.

Travel with us, Lord,
as we move towards this next stage of our commitment to you.
Feed us with your word,
deepen our prayer and our worship,
grant us the words and the actions of witness
and strengthen us as we live by the values of the kingdom.
Amen.

Welcome

The leader introduces the session.

Activity

In the confirmation service there is an opportunity for candidates to offer a 'testimony,' either spoken or written, telling something of their personal journey that has brought them to this point.

Spend five minutes on your own, noting key events, experiences, conversations, insights and anything else that has brought you to the commitment that confirmation signifies. Then share this with one other person and listen to their key points.

You have reflected on where you are and what has brought you to this point. As a group, explore your hopes and dreams for the future, in terms of your knowledge, your witness and your service. What will you need to do, and what help will you need if those hopes and dreams are to be realised?

Input

We do not always know where our journey will take us. There can be no guarantees, even after preparation, of just how things will turn out. God can lead us in unexpected ways and call us to do things for him we had never thought possible. The important thing is to journey in faith, trusting the one who has called us.

Reading

> Now the Lord said to Abram, 'Go from your country and your kindred and your father's house to the land that I will show you. I will make you a great nation, and I will bless you, and make your name great, so that you will be a blessing.'
>
> *Genesis 12:1, 2*

> By faith Abraham obeyed when he was called to set out for a place that he was to receive as an inheritance; and he set out, not knowing where he was going.
>
> *Hebrews 11:8*

Activity

Growing and travelling have their pleasures, but they can also be demanding. It is like that with the Christian journey and growing in faith. To stay strong we need a 'discipline' of feeding on the Bible, meeting with God in prayer, and sharing in the life of worship and witness of the Church. 'Discipline' does not have to be a harsh word: it is to do with being a disciple.

Discuss in your group what such 'discipline' might look like, and then on your own make a note of the key points that you will seek to follow as your 'discipline'.

Reflection

One more step along the world I go,
one more step along the world I go,

from the old things to the new
keep me travelling along with you.

*And it's from the old I travel to the new,
keep me travelling along with you.*

Round the corners of the world I turn,
more and more about the world I learn.
all the new things that I see
you'll be looking at along with me.

As I travel through the bad and good,
keep me travelling the way I should.
Where I see no way to go,
you'll be telling me the way, I know.

Give me courage when the world is rough,
keep me loving though the world is tough.
Leap and sing in all I do,
keep me travelling along with you.

You are older than the world can be,
you are younger than the life in me.
Ever old and ever new,
keep me travelling along with you.

Sidney Carter (1915–2004)

Prayer

Heavenly Father,
watch over me in my travelling and my growing.
Lord Jesus,
be alongside me in my journey.
Holy Spirit,
support and encourage me in my life as a disciple.
Lord, bless us all, now and always.
Amen.